This book should be

SPURS

THE OFFICIAL COMIC STRIP HISTORY

BY BOB BOND

TOTTENHAM
HOTSPUR

Published by Vision Sports Publishing Limited in 2013

Vision Sports Publishing Ltd
19-23 High Street
Kingston upon Thames
Surrey
KT1 1LL
www.visionsp.co.uk

© Bob Bond

ISBN: 978-1909534-12-4

This book is an officially licensed publication

The views expressed in this book do not necessarily reflect the views, opinions or policies of Tottenham Hotspur Football Club, nor those of any persons connected with the same.

Tottenham Hotspur FC,
Bill Nicholson Way,
High Road,
N17 0AP
www.tottenhamhotspur.com

Art and script: Bob Bond
Cover artwork: Stephen Gulbis
Cover design: Neal Cobourne
Editor: Jim Drewett
Production Editor: John Murray

Printed in China by Hung Hing

A CIP Catalogue record for this book is available from the British Library

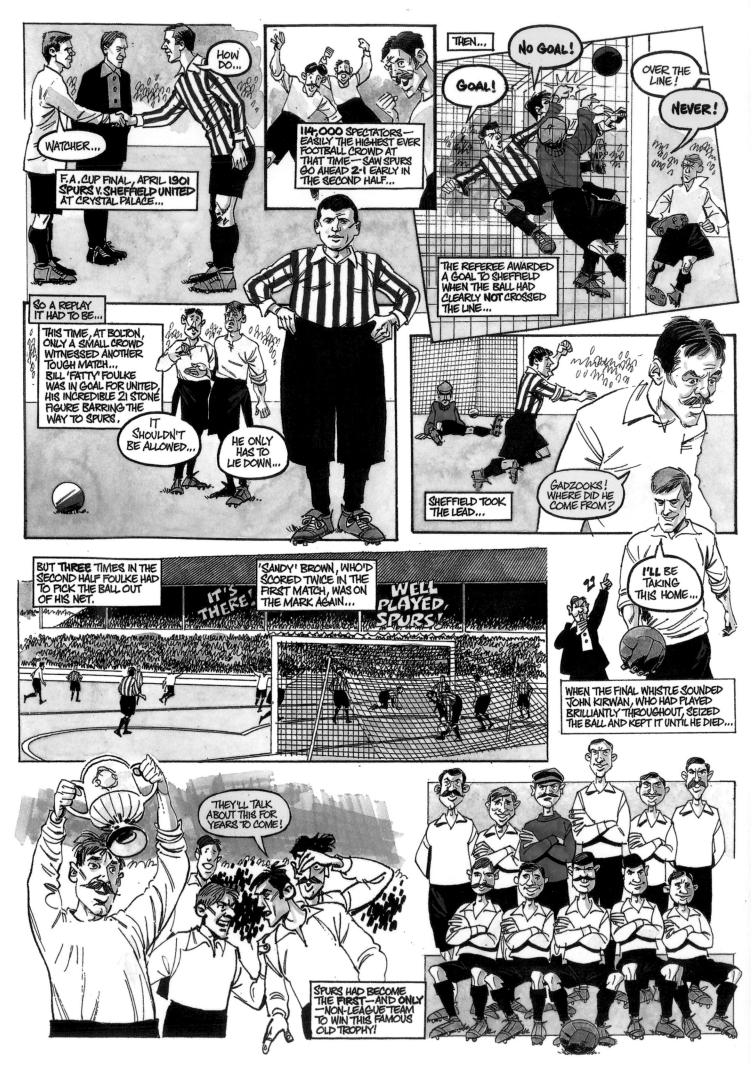

SPURS WON THE F.A. CUP AGAIN IN **1982**... THEY NEEDED ANOTHER REPLAY TO DEFEAT QUEEN'S PARK RANGERS, FOLLOWING A 1-1 DRAW. IT WAS A PENALTY KICK BY HODDLE WHICH SETTLED IT.

GOALKEEPER **RAY CLEMENCE**, SIGNED FROM LIVERPOOL, KEPT A CLEAN SHEET TO ADD ANOTHER WINNERS' MEDAL TO HIS ALREADY BIG COLLECTION...

1983-84 LOOKED LIKE BECOMING A VERY ORDINARY SEASON FOR SPURS, AS THEY HOVERED MID-TABLE AND WERE KNOCKED OUT OF BOTH DOMESTIC CUP COMPETITIONS IN THE EARLY ROUNDS...

BUT THEY'D QUALIFIED FOR THE UEFA CUP, AND AN EASY FIRST ROUND WIN OVER DROGHEDA AROUSED SOME OPTIMISM AMONG THE FANS...

HOW MANY IS THAT?

OVER TWO LEGS I RECKON WE ARE NOW 14 GOALS AHEAD...

PROGRESS IN LATER ROUNDS WAS NEVER THAT EASY, BUT A VITAL AWAY GOAL BY MARK FALCO AT HADJUK SPLIT GAVE THEM A CHANCE OF GOING THROUGH IN THE SEMI-FINAL...

...AND WHEN MICKEY HAZARD SCORED THE ONLY GOAL AT WHITE HART LANE, SPURS HAD MADE IT TO THE FINAL!

ALL THE TIES WERE OVER TWO MATCHES, HOME AND AWAY, INCLUDING THE FINAL AGAINST ANDERLECHT OF BELGIUM.

BUT AFTER EXTRA-TIME AT WHITE HART LANE...

SPURS DREW THE FIRST LEG THIS EVENING IN ANDERLECHT 1-1, MAKING THEM STRONG FAVOURITES TO LIFT THE CUP.

1-1 AGAIN... WHAT HAPPENS NOW?

IT'S DOWN TO PENALTIES!

STEVE ARCHIBALD MADE IT 4-2 TO SPURS IN THE SHOOT-OUT,... THE SCORE BECAME 4-3, WITH ONE BELGIAN KICK REMAINING!

IN **1989**
GARY LINEKER
WAS BOUGHT
FROM BARCELONA.

1991... THE FIRST YEAR
OF THE DECADE — COULD
IT BE SPURS' YEAR ONCE
AGAIN? THEIR FANS
SUPERSTITIOUSLY HELD
ON TO THAT BELIEF...

IT'S OUR
YEAR AGAIN...
YOU CAN BET
YOUR HOUSE
ON IT!

SPURS MET THEIR NORTH
LONDON RIVALS IN THE
F.A. CUP SEMI-FINAL.

JUST DON'T
BOTHER TRYING,
DAVID...

THE MATCH WAS PLAYED AT
WEMBLEY, AND WAS MADE
MEMORABLE BY A
GASCOIGNE FREE-KICK,
WHICH SCREAMED PAST
DAVID SEAMAN...

DID
YOU SEE
THAT?

TWO MORE GOALS
FROM LINEKER
SEALED THE WIN,
AND A PLACE IN
THE FINAL...

OUCH...

AAARGH!

THE F.A. CUP FINAL **1991**
SPURS v. NOTTINGHAM FOREST
AT WEMBLEY STADIUM...

UNACCOUNTABLY GASCOIGNE
THE HERO TURNED INTO A
VILLAIN, HIS BADLY MISTIMED
TACKLE INJURED HIS OPPONENT
AND HIMSELF, AND HE TOOK NO
FURTHER PART IN THE MATCH.

TO COMPOUND HIS
MISTAKE, STUART
PEARCE SCORED
FROM THE FREE-KICK...

SPURS FOUGHT
BACK...

GOAL!
STEWART
HAS SCORED!

IN EXTRA-TIME
ANOTHER BIZARRE
OWN GOAL SETTLED
THE MATCH... FOREST'S
DES WALKER HEADED
PAST HIS OWN GOALIE!

PAUL GASCOIGNE
NEVER PLAYED FOR
SPURS AGAIN,
WHEN FIT, HE
JOINED LAZIO
FOR £5 MILLION,
BUT FOR THREE
YEARS HE'D GIVEN
GREAT PLEASURE
TO SPURS FANS...

TEDDY SHERINGHAM AND DARREN ANDERTON CELEBRATE A GOAL IN 1995. TEDDY SCORED 96 TIMES IN FIVE SEASONS WITH SPURS BEFORE JOINING MANCHESTER UNITED IN 1997. AFTER GREAT SUCCESS AT OLD TRAFFORD, SHERINGHAM RETURNED TO SPURS TO NOTCH UP HIS 100TH GOAL FOR THE CLUB. HE HAS PLAYED MANY TIMES WITH DISTINCTION FOR ENGLAND, AS HAS ANDERTON...

IN 1994 SPURS SIGNED GERMAN INTERNATIONAL JURGEN KLINSMANN FOR £2 MILLION. HE HAD A REPUTATION FOR 'DIVING' IN THE BOX...SO THE FIRST TIME HE SCORED FOR SPURS HE DIVED FULL-LENGTH ON TO THE GRASS!

AFTER JUST ONE SEASON HE WENT BACK TO BAYERN MUNICH, BUT RETURNED TO SPURS FOR A BRIEF SPELL IN 1998, HELPING THEM AVOID THE THREAT OF RELEGATION.

LES FERDINAND BECAME A FIRM FAVOURITE AT SPURS AFTER HIS MOVE FROM NEWCASTLE IN 1997. LONDON-BORN LES IS GOOD IN THE AIR AND ON THE GROUND, FREQUENTLY STICKING THE BALL INTO THE NET WHEN REQUIRED...

FRENCH STAR DAVID GINOLA THRILLED THE FANS DURING HIS SHORT CAREER AT SPURS, OFTEN COMPLETING A DAZZLING RUN WITH AN UNSTOPPABLE SHOT...

TROPHIES WERE FEW AND FAR BETWEEN, BUT A GOAL FROM ALLAN NIELSEN WON THE FOOTBALL LEAGUE CUP IN 1999. DEEP INTO INJURY TIME HE BROKE LEICESTER CITY HEARTS WHEN HE DIVED TO HEAD THE BALL HOME, GEORGE GRAHAM WAS MANAGER AT THE TIME...

BUT 27 YEARS AFTER FIRST JOINING SPURS AS A PLAYER, GLENN HODDLE RETURNED IN 2001 AS MANAGER, BRINGING WITH HIM NEW HOPES AND ASPIRATIONS FOR THIS GREAT CLUB. THE SECOND CENTURY MAY WELL BE MORE MOMENTOUS THAN THE FIRST...

NEIL SULLIVAN JOINED SPURS FROM WIMBLEDON, SOON BECOMING FIRST CHOICE IN GOAL AND PLAYING SO WELL THAT THE FANS VOTED HIM PLAYER OF THE SEASON AT THE END OF HIS FIRST CAMPAIGN. SCOTLAND MADE SULLIVAN THEIR NUMBER ONE 'KEEPER...

THE BEST PERFORMANCE OF **2001-2002** CAME IN THE SECOND LEG OF THEIR LEAGUE CUP SEMI-FINAL AGAINST CHELSEA... HAVING LOST THE FIRST MATCH AT STAMFORD BRIDGE...

WE DIDN'T DESERVE TO LOSE TONIGHT...

GLENN HODDLE HAD TO PICK UP HIS MEN FOR THE RETURN MATCH AT TOTTENHAM...

WE PLAYED WELL AT CHELSEA, AND WE'RE ONLY ONE BEHIND, KEEP PLAYING FOOTBALL AND THE GOALS WILL COME...

AND DID THEY COME! **STEFFEN IVERSEN**, IN THE SECOND MINUTE... 1-0!

TIM SHERWOOD, FROM DARREN ANDERTON'S CORNER!

TEDDY SHERINGHAM, WITH A SWEET VOLLEY... **3-0**!!!

CHELSEA, FIRM FAVOURITES BEFORE THE MATCH STARTED, WERE DOWN AND OUT, THEIR FANS DRIFTED OFF HOME LONG BEFORE THE END, **SIMON DAVIES**... 4-0!

AND AS **SERGEI REBROV** STUCK IN THE FIFTH IT WAS ALREADY CLEAR THAT SPURS, NOT CHELSEA WERE ON THE WAY TO CARDIFF....

SPURS PAID £11 MILLION FOR REBROV (LEFT), A STRIKER FROM THE UKRAINE, IT WAS A CLUB RECORD FEE...

SPURS LOST TO BLACKBURN IN THE FINAL... IF ONLY GUS POYET'S SHOT HAD BEEN A FEW INCHES TO THE RIGHT...

IF ONLY A PENALTY HAD BEEN AWARDED TO SPURS WHEN TEDDY SHERINGHAM WAS CLEARLY TRIPPED IN THE BOX...

LEDLEY KING (ABOVE) EMERGED AS ONE OF THE BEST YOUNG DEFENDERS IN THE COUNTRY, GOING ON TO STAR FOR BOTH SPURS AND ENGLAND...

YOUNG MIDFIELDER **SIMON DAVIES** COST SPURS £700,000 FROM PETERBOROUGH IN JANUARY **2000**, AFTER SCORING TWICE ON HIS FA CUP DEBUT FOR THE CLUB, DAVIES JUST GOT BETTER AND BETTER AND WOULD GO ON TO PLAY MORE THAN **100** GAMES FOR SPURS...

ONCE AGAIN, ALL DEPENDED ON THEIR FINAL MATCH, ON A SUNDAY...

IF SPURS, A POINT AHEAD OF THEIR ARCH-RIVALS ARSENAL, WIN AT WEST HAM TOMORROW, THEY WILL QUALIFY FOR A PLACE IN THE CHAMPIONS LEAGUE...

IT WAS SATURDAY EVENING AT THEIR FAVOURITE HOTEL...

GET A GOOD NIGHT'S SLEEP TONIGHT LADS, THIS IS OUR BIGGEST GAME FOR YEARS...

BUT...

?

IN OTHER ROOMS...

HEY UP... LET ME GET TO THAT TOILET!

OOOH...

NEXT MORNING...

SORRY BOSS, BUT KEANO IS UNWELL, TOO. HE'S THROWING UP SOMETHING TERRIBLE...

VIRTUALLY THE WHOLE TEAM HAD BEEN STRUCK DOWN BY A VIRUS!

THEY CAN'T EVEN STAND UP... WE'LL HAVE TO ASK FOR A POSTPONEMENT

WEST HAM WOULD HAVE AGREED TO THIS, BUT WHEN ASKED THE PREMIER LEAGUE EXECUTIVE WAS IN A QUANDARY...

IF YOU DON'T PLAY, WE WOULD HAVE TO HOLD AN ENQUIRY...

...IN WHICH CASE WE MIGHT HAVE TO DEDUCT POINTS FROM YOU ANYWAY.

SOME OF THE SICK HAD TO TURN OUT...

WE'LL HAVE TO PLAY, LADS... EVEN WITH A BELOW-STRENGTH TEAM.

TIE UP MY BOOTLACES, WILL YOU?

MEANWHILE ARSENAL, THE ONLY TEAM WHO COULD CATCH SPURS, WERE PLAYING WIGAN...

THE UPTON PARK CROWD LET THE PLAYERS KNOW WHAT WAS HAPPENING AT HIGHBURY...

1-0 TO THE ARSENAL!

DEFOE SCORED AGAINST HIS FORMER TEAM, BUT IN THE SECOND HALF SPURS UNDERSTANDABLY WILTED...

IT WAS A BRAVE EFFORT, BUT...

GOAL!

FOR WEST HAM!

ARSENAL'S WIN ENABLED THEM TO LEAPFROG THE DEFEATED SPURS...

THE 2011-12 SEASON BEGAN CATASTROPHICALLY, WITH HEAVY DEFEATS BY THE TWO MANCHESTER SIDES...

PLAYED TWO... LOST TWO...

NOT LOOKING GOOD...

BUT SPURS THEN WON **TEN** OF THEIR NEXT ELEVEN LEAGUE GAMES!

4-0!

...AFTER WHICH SPURS WERE RARELY OUT OF THE TOP FOUR.

TAKE THAT, LIVERPOOL!

BENOIT ASSOU-EKOTTO

VAN DER VAART SCORED IN FIVE SUCCESSIVE PREMIER LEAGUE MATCHES...

...AND GARETH BALE WAS HITTING THE NET REGULARLY WITH SOME WONDER GOALS.

A PREMIER LEAGUE DEFEAT AT QPR WAS DAMAGING TO THEIR CHANCES...

WE'RE DOWN TO FIFTH PLACE...

THREE BEHIND NEWCASTLE...

TO FINISH FOURTH SPURS **HAD** TO WIN THEIR LAST MATCH...

...AND DID!

IT WAS IN THE F.A. CUP QUARTER-FINAL AGAINST BOLTON WHEN FABRICE MUAMBA COLLAPSED WITH A CARDIAC ARREST, AND THE GAME HAD TO BE ABANDONED.

THANKFULLY THE POPULAR MUAMBA SURVIVED. SPURS WON THE REPLAYED MATCH... BUT WHEN THE REFEREE AWARDED CHELSEA THE GOAL THAT NEVER WAS, IT WAS CLEAR THAT SPURS WERE NOT GOING TO WIN THE SEMI-FINAL...

GOAL!

NO GOAL...

BUT IT DIDN'T CROSS THE LINE, REF!

WITH MODRIC AND VAN DER VAART GONE, SPURS FANS MUST HAVE WONDERED WHAT 2012-13 HAD IN STORE...